Garden Fresh Recipes

Wal-Mart Associates provide assistance to various charitable organizations across this great country. One of the worthy causes that Wal-Mart Associates gives assistance to is the Children's Miracle Network. There are many, many other causes that Wal-Mart Associates assist with, including aiding the homeless, fire victims, flood relief, and so forth. By the purchase of this book, you are aiding the Wal-Mart Associates of your community in reaching their goal to provide assistance to their specific cause.

Thank You.

1995

Printed on recycled paper in the United States of America by
KEEPSAKE COOKBOOKS • FUNDCO PRINTERS
1815 Wayne Road - Savannah, TN 38372
1-800-426-9827

Table of Contents

Appetizers and Beverages

CHEESY NACHOS

1 cup Monterey Jack cheese
   with jalapeño peppers,
   shredded
1 cup sharp Cheddar cheese,
   shredded

1 small onion, chopped
1 package nacho chips

Place chips on cookie sheet. Sprinkle cheese and onion over chips. Bake at 350° until cheese melts, about 10 minutes. 8 to 10 servings.

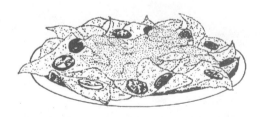

PINEAPPLE CHEESE BALL

1 (8-ounce) can crushed
  pineapple, drained
2 (8-ounce) packages cream
  cheese, softened
2 teaspoons onion, finely
  chopped

2 teaspoons bell pepper, finely
  chopped
2 cups pecans, chopped
1 1/2 teaspoons seasoned salt

Beat cheese until smooth. Add onion, pepper, pineapple, salt and 1 cup pecans. Shape into ball and roll in remaining pecans. Chill for 2 hours before serving. 10 to 12 servings.

BROCCOLI CHEESE DIP

1 package frozen broccoli,
  chopped
1 package Mexican pasteurized
  process cheese spread

1 (8-ounce) package cream
  cheese

Cook broccoli according to directions on box. Melt the cheeses and stir in broccoli. 14 to 16 servings.

MEXICAN DIP

2 pounds pasteurized process
   cheese spread
1 can tomatoes with green
   chilies

1/2 cup milk
1/2 pound ground beef
1/2 pound mild sausage
1 small onion, diced

Brown ground beef, sausage and onion in a skillet. Melt cheese and milk in microwave and combine all ingredients in a large bowl. Serve with nacho chips. 10 to 12 servings.

FRUIT DIP

2 (8 ounce) packages cream
   cheese, softened
1 (8 ounce) sour cream

1/2 box confectioners sugar
Juice of one orange

Blend above and add confectioners sugar to taste. Add more sugar if needed. Chill and serve with fruit. 10 to 12 servings.

FRUIT TEA

1 (6 ounce) can frozen orange
   juice, thawed
1 (6 ounce) can frozen
   lemonade, thawed
6 regular size tea bags or 3
   family size

1 1/2 cups sugar
4 cups boiling water
10 cups water

Place tea bags in boiling water and let stand for 8 minutes. Dissolve the sugar in the hot tea and add remaining ingredients. Store in refrigerator and serve cold over ice. Yield: 1 gallon.

SUMMERTIME PUNCH

2 1/2 cups pineapple juice
1 (6 ounce) can frozen orange
   juice, thawed

1 (12 ounce) can apricot nectar
1 (6 ounce) can frozen
   lemonade, thawed

Mix orange juice and lemonade according to directions on cans. Add the remaining ingredients. Chill and serve. 20 (1/2 cup) servings.

SOFT DRINK PUNCH

1 (6 ounce) can frozen
   lemonade, thawed
1 (46 ounce) can pineapple
   juice

2 envelopes unsweetened soft
   drink mix, any flavor
2 cups sugar
10 cups water

Combine all ingredients. Chill. 35 (1/2) cup servings.

STRAWBERRY SHAKE

1 (10 ounce) package frozen
   strawberries or 1 1/4 cups
   fresh strawberries
1 cup cold milk

1 cup cold orange juice
1/2 to 3/4 cup vanilla ice cream
Whipped cream

Mix all ingredients, except whipped cream, together in blender. Blend for 25 seconds. Pour into dessert dishes or glasses. Top with whipped cream. 4 servings.

NOTES

Breads

YEAST ROLLS

1 package dry yeast
2 cups lukewarm water
1/4 cup sugar
4 cups self-rising flour

1 egg
1/2 teaspoon salt
3/4 cup melted shortening

Dissolve yeast in water. Add all ingredients, except flour and mix well.
Dump in flour. Mix thoroughly. Store in refrigerator covered. When
ready to cook, spoon into well greased tins. Do not let rise. Bake at 425°
for 20 to 25 minutes. Yields: 2 dozen.

QUICK ROLLS

1 cup self-rising flour
1/2 cup milk

1/4 cup salad dressing
1 tablespoon sugar

Combine all ingredients and pour into greased muffin tins. Bake at 425°
for 15 minutes or until brown on top. Yields: 12 muffins.

PIZZA DOUGH

1 cup warm water
1 teaspoon salt
2 tablespoons oil

2 1/2 cups all-purpose flour
1 teaspoon sugar
1 package yeast

Mix water and yeast together. Add all ingredients together in a medium bowl and mix well using hands. Place dough in a warm place for 10 minutes. Press out on pizza pan and add toppings. Yields: 1 pizza crust.

ANGEL BISCUITS

2 packages dry yeast
3/4 cup salad oil
1/2 cup warm water
3 teaspoons baking powder
2 cups buttermilk

1 1/4 teaspoons soda
3 tablespoons sugar
2 teaspoons salt
5 cups plain flour (3 cups
white/2 cups whole wheat)

Sift dry ingredients together in large bowl. Dissolve yeast in warm water and add oil and buttermilk. Pour liquid ingredients over flour mixture. Store in refrigerator until ready to use. Roll out as needed and bake at 400° for 15 to 20 minutes. Yields: 3 to 4 dozen.

BROCCOLI CORNBREAD

1 box cornbread mix
1 stick margarine
1 (10 ounce) package chopped,
   frozen broccoli

3/4 cup sour cream
3 eggs
1/4 cup Cheddar cheese, grated

Cook broccoli and drain. Melt margarine and mix all ingredients together. Pour into greased 9x13-inch baking dish. Cook at 350° for 40 minutes or until toothpick comes out clean. 6 to 8 servings

MEXICAN CORNBREAD

1 cup corn meal
1 cup cream-style corn
1 small can chopped green
   chili peppers
1 cup Cheddar cheese, grated

1/2 teaspoon salt
1/2 teaspoon soda
2/3 cup buttermilk
2 eggs
1/3 cup oil

Mix all ingredients together. Pour into well greased skillet or muffin tins. Bake at 375° for 40 minutes. Yield: 12 muffins.

HUSH PUPPIES

3 cups corn meal
1/2 cup all-purpose flour
4 teaspoons baking powder
11/2 teaspoons salt

1 teaspoon black pepper
11/2 cups buttermilk
1 cup finely chopped onions
2 eggs, slightly beaten

Combine all dry ingredients together in large bowl. Add buttermilk, onions and eggs. Drop by tablespoonful into deep hot oil and fry until golden brown. Yields: 2 dozen.

SQUASH PUPPIES

2 cups fresh squash, grated
1 egg
1/4 cup chopped onion
1/2 cup self-rising cornmeal

6 tablespoons all-purpose
  flour
1 teaspoon sugar
Salt and pepper to taste

Mix together and drop by tablespoon into hot oil and fry until golden brown. Yields: 2 dozen.

PECAN MUFFINS

1/3 cup margarine, melted
2 eggs, beaten
1 cup brown sugar

1/2 cup self-rising flour
1 teaspoon vanilla extract
1 cup pecans, chopped

Combine all the ingredients in a mixing bowl and stir well. Bake at 350° for 20 minutes in greased muffin pan. Yields: 12 muffins.

HONEY RAISIN BRAN MUFFINS

1 1/4 cups all-purpose flour
1/4 teaspoon salt
1 tablespoon baking powder
1 cup milk
1/3 cup honey

1 egg
3 tablespoons vegetable oil
2 1/2 cups bran cereal with
    raisins

Mix together cereal, milk, honey, oil and egg, stirring well. Sift together flour, salt and baking powder. Add to cereal mixture. Stir only until combined. Pour into greased muffin pan. Bake at 400° for 18 to 20 minutes. Yields: 12 muffins.

BANANA MUFFINS

1/2 cup margarine	1/4 teaspoon salt
1 cup sugar	1 teaspoon nutmeg
1 egg	1 1/2 cups all-purpose flour
1 teaspoon soda	2 or 3 mashed bananas
1 tablespoon cold water	1/2 cup nuts, chopped

Cream margarine and sugar together in mixing bowl. Add egg. Dissolve soda in water and add to mixture. Fold in dry ingredients. Add the bananas to the above mixture and pour into greased muffin pan. Bake at 350° for 20 minutes. Yields: 12 muffins.

BREAKFAST COFFEE CAKE

2 sticks margarine
2 cups sugar
1 pint sour cream
4 eggs

2 teaspoons baking soda
3 cups all-purpose flour
2 teaspoons vanilla extract

TOPPING:
1/2 cup sugar
1/2 cup brown sugar

1/2 cup chopped nuts
1 teaspoon cinnamon

Cream together margarine, sugar and eggs. Add sour cream and vanilla. Fold in dry ingredients. Pour into 2 (8-inch) square greased cake pans, 1/2 of the batter. Sprinkle with 2/3 of the topping. Put remainder of batter over topping and top with topping mixture. Bake at 350° for 35 minutes. Can be frozen. Yields: 2 coffee cakes.

STRAWBERRY BREAD

1 1/2 cups all-purpose flour	1 cup sugar
1/2 teaspoon salt	2 eggs, beaten
1/2 teaspoon baking soda	1/2 cup oil
1 1/2 teaspoons cinnamon	1 cup strawberries, chopped

Mix dry ingredients in medium bowl. In small bowl, stir together eggs, oil, and strawberries. Pour over dry mixture and mix well. Pour into greased and floured 5x9 inch loaf pan and bake at 350° for 1 hour or until toothpick comes out clean. Yields: 1 loaf.

BANANA NUT BREAD

3 bananas
1 teaspoon baking soda
1/2 cup margarine
1 cup sugar

3 eggs
2 cups all-purpose flour
1/2 teaspoon salt
1/2 cup nuts, chopped

In small bowl, mash bananas and add soda. Allow to stand while mixing remaining ingredients. Blend together margarine, sugar and eggs. Add banana mixture. Mix together flour and salt and fold into above mixture. Stir in nuts. Bake at 325° in a greased and floured loaf pan for 1 hour or until toothpick comes out clean. Yields: 1 loaf.

POPPY SEED BREAD

3 eggs
21/2 cups sugar
11/2 cups milk
11/4 cups oil
1 tablespoon poppy seeds
11/2 teaspoons baking powder

11/2 teaspoons salt
11/2 teaspoons vanilla extract
11/2 teaspoons almond
   flavoring
3 cups all-purpose flour

In large mixing bowl, cream together eggs and sugar. Add the milk and oil and stir well. Add all remaining ingredients and mix well. Batter will be thin. Pour batter into two greased and floured loaf pans and bake at 325° for 1 hour and 10 minutes. While bread is still warm glaze.

GLAZE:
3/4 cup sugar
11/4 cups orange juice
1/2 teaspoon vanilla extract

1/2 teaspoon almond flavoring
2 tablespoons margarine

Cook over medium heat until sugar dissolves. Pour over warm bread. Makes 2 loaves.

DOUGHNUT BALLS

2 cups all-purpose flour	1 teaspoon baking powder
1/4 cup sugar	1/4 cup oil
1 teaspoon salt	3/4 cup milk
1 teaspoon nutmeg	1 egg

In a medium bowl mix together flour, sugar, salt, baking powder and nutmeg. In a small bowl mix together oil, milk and egg. Pour the liquid mixture over the dry ingredients and stir well. Drop by teaspoonfuls into deep, hot oil. Cook about 2 minutes or until golden brown. Drain the balls on paper towel. Roll warm balls in confectioners sugar or mix up a confectioner sugar glaze with milk and vanilla extract. Makes about 2 1/2 dozen balls.

NOTES

Salads and Side Dishes

LAYERED SALAD

1 medium lettuce head
1/2 cup celery
1/2 cup green pepper
1/2 cup onion, chopped
1 (10-ounce) package frozen
   peas, thawed
3/4 cup salad dressing

3/4 cup sour cream
1 tablespoon sugar
1 1/2 cups Cheddar cheese,
   shredded
8 slices bacon, crisply fried and
   crumbled

Break lettuce into bite-size pieces and layer in a 13x9x2-inch dish. Combine celery, green pepper, onion and peas and spoon over lettuce. Blend together sour cream and salad dressing. Spread over second layer. Sprinkle with sugar. Top with cheese and bacon. Cover; refrigerate overnight. 10 servings.

MACARONI SALAD

2 packages twist macaroni	1 large bell pepper
1 1/2 cups sugar	2 carrots
1 cup vinegar	2 cups mayonnaise
1 large onion	

Cook and drain macaroni. Mix sugar and vinegar in small saucepan and bring to a boil. Set aside and cool. Grate onion, bell pepper and carrot and mix with mayonnaise. Mix with cooled macaroni mixture and stir well. Store in refrigerator in airtight container overnight before serving. 10 servings.

TACO SALAD

1 head lettuce
1 onion
1 can kidney beans
1 avocado
1 package nacho chips
4 tomatoes, chopped

4 ounces Cheddar cheese,
   grated
8 ounce bottle French dressing
1 pound ground beef
Taco sauce (to taste)

Brown ground beef and onion together. Add drained kidney beans to beef mixture and simmer for 10 minutes. Cool beef mixture and prepare rest of ingredients. Mix French dressing and taco sauce together and pour over salad. Crumble nachos on top. 6 to 8 servings.

ORANGE SALAD

1 large tub whipped topping
1 (3-ounce) orange Jello
1 pint cottage cheese
1 small can mandarin oranges,
    drained

1 small can crushed pineapple,
    drained

Mix whipped topping and dry Jello together. Add cottage cheese, oranges and pineapple. Chill. 8 servings.

CHERRY FRUIT SALAD

1 can cherry pie filling
1 can pineapple chunks,
    drained

1 or 2 cans mandarin oranges,
    drained
2 to 4 bananas, cut in chunks

Mix together and chill. 6 to 8 servings.

FRUIT SALAD

1 cup fresh or frozen
  strawberries
1 can chunk pineapple, drained
1 can mandarin oranges, drained

3 bananas
1 package lemon or vanilla
  instant pudding

Drain fruit and save juice. Mix juice with instant pudding. Pour over fruit. Chill. 6 to 8 servings.

FIVE CUP SALAD

1 cup chunky pineapple
1 cup mandarin oranges
1 cup coconut

1 cup miniature marshmallows
1 cup sour cream

Drain fruit and mix all ingredients together in a medium size bowl. 6 servings.

ORANGE SHERBET SALAD

1 (6-ounce) package orange
   Jello
1 cup boiling water
1 pint orange sherbet
1 cup miniature marshmallows

1 can mandarin oranges,
   drained
1 (8 1/4 ounce) can crushed
   pineapple, drained
1 (8 ounce) whipped topping

Dissolve Jello in water; add sherbet and stir until melted. Add
marshmallows and allow to cool. Add oranges and pineapple. Fold in
whipped topping. Spoon into individual molds or 5-cup mold; freeze. 8
to 10 servings.

FROZEN SALAD

1 can sweetened condensed milk	1 small can crushed pineapple
1 can cherry pie filling	1 small bowl whipped topping

Mix all ingredients together in medium bowl. Pour into 13x9x2-inch glass pan and freeze. Serve on lettuce leaves. Makes 15 (2 1/2-inch) squares.

BROCCOLI SALAD

3 bunches broccoli	1 cup green grapes
1 cup celery, chopped	1 cup red grapes
1/8 cup onion, finely chopped	1 cup raisins
1/3 cup sunflower seeds	1 cup bacon bits
1 cup salad dressing	

Mix together all ingredients in a large bowl and toss lightly. Chill and serve. 12 to 14 servings.

COLE SLAW

1 head cabbage, shredded
1 large onion, sliced and
    separated
1 cup oil
1 cup vinegar

3/4 cup sugar
1 1/2 teaspoons mustard
1 1/2 teaspoons salt
1/2 teaspoon celery seed

Layer cabbage and onion in a large bowl. Boil remaining ingredients and pour over cabbage and onion mixture while hot. Cover and refrigerate overnight. 10 to 12 servings.

CUCUMBER SALAD

3 medium cucumbers, sliced
    thin
1/2 cup sour cream

1/4 cup vinegar
1 medium onion, sliced
Salt and pepper

Cover cucumbers in salt; let stand 1 hour. Squeeze all juice from cucumbers. Add onion, sour cream and vinegar; add pepper. 4 servings.

VEGETABLE SALAD

1/4 cup oil
3/4 cup vinegar
1/2 teaspoon pepper

1/2 teaspoon salt
3/4 cup sugar

Combine all the above ingredients in a medium pot and bring to a boil. Set aside and let cool.

1 can shoe peg corn, drained
1 can small green peas, drained
1 can French style green beans, drained

1 can pimentos, drained
1 cup onion, chopped
1 cup celery, chopped
1 cup green peppers, chopped

Mix together all the ingredients in a large bowl. Pour the boiled mixture over this and refrigerate. Will keep for 2 weeks. 10 to 12 servings.

POTATO SALAD

4 cups potatoes
3 eggs, hard boiled
1 small onion
1/4 cup sweet relish

2 tablespoons sugar
2 tablespoons mustard
1 cup salad dressing
Salt and pepper to taste

Peel and cube potatoes and boil until tender. Cool potatoes. In a large bowl combine all ingredients. Sprinkle with paprika. Refrigerate until ready to serve. 4 to 6 servings.

ENGLISH PEA SALAD

1 can English peas, drained
1 egg, hard boiled
3 tablespoons onion, chopped

1/4 cup salad dressing
Salt and pepper to taste

Mix all ingredients together and chill. 4 servings.

CORN SALAD

1 (12 ounce) can shoe peg
  corn, drained
1/4 cup green pepper, diced
2 tablespoons pimento,
  chopped
1/2 cup celery, finely chopped
1/2 cup sliced red onion,
  separated into rings

1 cup cucumber, diced
1/3 cup oil
3 tablespoons sugar
11/2 teaspoons salt
3 tablespoons red wine
  vinegar

Combine all vegetables. Mix oil, sugar, vinegar and salt. Stir until sugar dissolves. Pour over vegetables and toss . Chill overnight in refrigerator. Drain before serving. 4 to 6 servings.

FRUITED CHICKEN SALAD

3 cups cooked chicken
1 cup apples
3/4 cup celery
2 tablespoons green olives
1 cup pineapple, drained

2 eggs, hard boiled
2 tablespoons sweet pickle
1/2 cup raisins
1/2 cup slivered almonds
3/4 cup salad dressing

Chop first 7 ingredients. Add remaining ingredients. Mix well. Chill several hours. Serve on lettuce leaves. 4 to 6 servings.

STEWED TOMATOES

1 pint canned tomatoes
4 biscuits
2 tablespoons margarine

4 tablespoons sugar
Salt and pepper to taste

Put tomatoes in small saucepan. Add margarine, sugar, salt and pepper. Cook together for about 5 minutes. Break up biscuits into this mixture and stir until bread is saturated. Serve while hot. 2 to 4 servings.

BAKED BEANS

1/2 pound ground beef
3/4 pound bacon
2 (16 ounce) cans pork and beans
1 cup ketchup
1 small onion, chopped

1/4 cup brown sugar
1/4 cup barbecue sauce
1/4 cup green pepper, chopped
1 tablespoon Worcestershire sauce
1 tablespoon white vinegar

Cook and drain ground beef and bacon. Mix all ingredients together and bake at 350° for 1 hour. 6 to 8 servings.

MEXICAN BEANS

11/2 pounds ground beef
1 can pork and beans
1 can green lima
1 can kidney beans
3 tablespoons brown sugar

1 small onion
1 tablespoon mustard
1/2 cup ketchup
Chili powder to taste

Brown ground beef and onion together. Add all other ingredients and bake at 350° for 30 minutes. 4 to 6 servings.

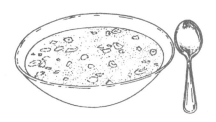

GREEN BEAN CASSEROLE

1 can French style green
   beans, drained
1 can whole kernel corn,
   drained
1/4 cup celery, chopped
1/2 cup onion, chopped
1/4 cup bell pepper, chopped

1 cup cheese, grated
1 carton sour cream
1 can mushroom soup
1/4 cup margarine, melted
1 stack of round butter
   flavored crackers, crumbled
1/4 cup almonds, chopped

Mix all ingredients except margarine, crackers, almonds. Pour into dish. Crumble crackers and mix with melted margarine. Sprinkle on top of casserole. Top with almonds and bake at 350° for 45 minutes. 4 servings.

SWEET AND SOUR GREEN BEANS

1 can green beans
3 slices bacon, fried and
    crumbled
2 tablespoons margarine
1/4 cup onion, chopped

1 tablespoon mustard
2 tablespoons vinegar
2 tablespoons brown sugar
Salt and pepper to taste

Place beans in medium pot. In a skillet cook onions in margarine. Add mustard, brown sugar and vinegar. Pour sauce over beans and simmer on low for 2 hours. When ready to serve, stir the beans and sauce together. Sprinkle bacon over the mixture. 4 servings.

BROCCOLI CASSEROLE

1 package frozen broccoli,
   chopped
1/2 cup rice, cooked
1/2 cup onion

1/2 stick margarine, melted
1/2 cup Cheddar cheese, grated
1/2 cup milk
1/2 can cream of chicken soup

Cook broccoli according to directions on package. Combine all ingredients in a 2 quart casserole dish and cook for one hour at 275°. 4 to 6 servings.

POTATO CASSEROLE

4 to 6 medium size potatoes
1 medium onion, sliced

1 stick margarine, melted
Salt and pepper to taste

Cut potatoes into quarters and cut again. In a 13x9x2-inch pan layer potatoes and onions. Pour melted butter over mixture. Season with salt and pepper. Bake at 350° for 1 hour covered with foil. Remove foil and brown for the last 5 minutes. 4 to 6 servings.

AU GRATIN POTATOES

6 medium potatoes
1/4 cup margarine
1 teaspoon salt
2 cups Cheddar cheese,
    shredded

1/2 cup onion, chopped
1 tablespoon flour
1/4 teaspoon pepper
2 cups milk

Cut potatoes into thin slices. In a saucepan, cook onion in margarine until tender. Stir in flour, salt and pepper. Cook over low heat, stirring constantly. Remove from heat and stir in milk and 1 1/2 cups of cheese. Heat to boiling and boil for 1 minute. Place potatoes in ungreased 4 quart casserole and pour cheese sauce over potatoes. Cook uncovered at 350° for 1 hour. Sprinkle remaining cheese on top and bake until melted. 4 to 6 servings.

ASPARAGUS CASSEROLE

1 can asparagus, drained
1 can mushroom soup
1/2 stick margarine
1 cup cheese, grated
2 hard boiled eggs, sliced

1 can English peas, drained
1 cup cracker crumbs
1/2 teaspoon salt
1 small can pimento, diced

Pour asparagus, peas and soup into a 4 quart baking dish. Add hard boiled eggs, diced pimento and salt. Add melted margarine to cracker crumbs and sprinkle on top of the casserole. Garnish top of casserole with grated cheese. Place in 350° oven and bake for 45 minutes. 4 to 6 servings.

SQUASH CASSEROLE

2 cups cooked squash
1/4 cup onion
1 egg, beaten

1 can cream of chicken soup
1/4 cup margarine
1 cup bread stuffing

Cook squash and onion together until tender. Drain. Mix in beaten egg and soup. Melt 1/4 cup of margarine in 8x8-inch casserole dish; put 2/3 cup of the bread stuffing in bottom of dish. Pour squash mixture over the stuffing. Put remaining stuffing on top of casserole. Bake at 325° for 25 minutes. 4 servings.

EASTER CASSEROLE

1 pound mild sausage
3 tablespoons onions, chopped
3 tablespoons bell pepper,
    chopped

1/2 cup sour cream
6 eggs, slightly beaten
Salt and pepper to taste

In a large skillet, brown sausage, onions and bell pepper. Drain. In a medium baking dish, layer sausage, reserving 1/4 of the mixture for topping. Mix eggs and sour cream and pour over sausage. Bake at 350° until eggs are semi-set. Stir mixture and top with remaining sausage. Bake until eggs are done. 4 to 6 servings.

EGGPLANT CASSEROLE

2 large eggplants
1 tablespoon margarine
1 large onion
2 eggs, beaten

2 cups Cheddar cheese,
  shredded
Buttered bread crumbs

Peel eggplant and cut into slices. Boil in salted water until tender. Drain
and mash. Chop onion and sauté in margarine. Combine other
ingredients and top casserole with buttered bread crumbs. Bake at 350°
for 30 minutes. 4 to 6 servings.

PARMESAN POTATOES

6 medium potatoes
1/4 cup all-purpose flour
1/2 teaspoon salt

1/2 teaspoon pepper
1/4 cup Parmesan cheese
1/3 cup margarine

Peel potatoes and cut into quarters. Combine flour, cheese, salt and pepper in a plastic bag. Place a few pieces of potatoes in the bag at a time and shake. Melt margarine in a 13x9x2-inch baking dish. Place potatoes in a single layer in dish. Bake at 350° for 1 hour, turning once during baking. 4 to 6 servings.

MEXICAN POTATOES

6 to 8 medium potatoes
1 onion, chopped
1 green pepper, chopped
1 pound pasteurized process
   cheese spread, cubed

1 can diced tomatoes with
   green chilies
4 tablespoons margarine

Boil potatoes whole until done; cool and slice. Layer in 13x9x2-inch casserole dish. Sauté onion and green pepper in margarine. Add cheese and tomatoes. Stir together until melted. Pour over potatoes and bake at 350° for 20 minutes or until bubbly. 4 to 6 servings.

MAC 'N CHEESE

2 cups (7 ounces) elbow
  macaroni
1/4 cup green pepper, chopped
1/2 cup onion, chopped

2 tablespoons margarine
1/2 cup milk
1 pound pasteurized process
  cheese spread, cubed

Cook macaroni according to directions on package. Sauté green pepper
and onion in margarine. Reduce heat and add cheese and milk. Stir until
cheese is melted. Stir in macaroni. Spoon into a 2 quart baking dish.
Bake at 350° for 15 minutes. 6 servings.

SPANISH RICE

1 small onion, chopped	1 1/2 cups water
1 green pepper, chopped	1 teaspoon salt
1 1/2 cups uncooked quick rice	1 teaspoon sugar
1/3 cup oil	1/4 teaspoon pepper
2 (8 ounce) cans tomato sauce	1 teaspoon lemon juice

Sauté onion, green pepper and rice in oil until rice is lightly browned.
Add the remaining ingredients; cover and bring to a boil. Reduce heat
and uncover. Simmer for 10 minutes. 4 to 6 servings.

ENGLISH PEA CASSEROLE

1 can green English peas
1 can cream of mushroom
    soup
2 boiled eggs, chopped

1 1/4 cups cheese, grated
1/4 cup margarine
Cracker crumbs for topping
    (saltines)

Cook peas in margarine for 10 minutes. In a medium bowl, mix all ingredients together and pour into a 2 quart casserole dish. Crush about 1/2 pack of saltine crackers and sprinkle on top. Bake at 350° for 30 minutes. 4 to 6 servings.

SWEET POTATOES

3 cups sweet potatoes
2 eggs
1 cup sugar
1/2 cup margarine

1 teaspoon vanilla extract
1/4 cup orange juice
1 teaspoon cinnamon

Slice potatoes and boil until tender. Drain and place in a shallow casserole dish. Pour orange juice over; sprinkle with sugar and cinnamon and dot with margarine. Bake at 350° for 30 minutes. 4 to 6 servings.

MARINATED VEGETABLES

1 can English peas, drained
1 can shoe peg corn, drained
1 can French green beans,
    drained

1 onion, chopped
2 stalks celery, chopped
1 green pepper, chopped
1 bottle Italian dressing

Mix all vegetables together in large bowl. Pour Italian dressing over the vegetables and toss lightly. Store covered in refrigerator for 2 days. Drain before serving. 10 servings.

BAKED APRICOTS

3 (29 ounce) cans whole
   apricots
1 cup brown sugar

1/4 cup margarine
1 cup Ritz crackers, crushed
1/2 teaspoon cinnamon

Drain apricots, remove pits and place in well buttered 13x9x2-inch glass dish. Mix brown sugar and cinnamon together and sprinkle over apricots. Pour the crushed crackers over this and dot with margarine. 4 to 6 servings.

NOTES

Main Dishes

CHICKEN AMANDINE

6 chicken breasts, skinned and
    boned
1 (10¾ ounce) can cream of
    chicken soup
1 cup sour cream
1 (10¾ ounce) can cream of
    mushroom soup
½ cup sliced almonds
Hot cooked rice or noodles

Place chicken breasts in 13x9x2-inch baking dish. Combine soups and pour over chicken. Spread sour cream on top. Sprinkle with almonds. Bake at 350° for 1½ hours. Serve over rice or noodles. 6 servings.

ORANGE-BAKED CHICKEN CASSEROLE

1 (2 1/2 to 3 pound) chicken,
   cut in pieces
1/2 cup flour
1 teaspoon salt
1/4 teaspoon pepper
1/3 cup margarine and
   vegetable oil combined

1 (6 ounce) can frozen orange
   juice concentrate, thawed
1/4 cup brown sugar
1 juice can water
1/2 teaspoon nutmeg
1 medium onion, thinly sliced
1 teaspoon oregano

Coat chicken with flour, salt and pepper. Heat margarine and oil in large skillet. Brown chicken. Place in buttered 13x9x2-inch casserole. Combine remaining ingredients. Pour over chicken. Cover and bake at 350° for 1 hour. Serve with noodles or rice. 6 servings.

SOUR CREAM CHICKEN ENCHILADA

2 cans cream of chicken soup
1 cup (8 ounces) sour cream
2 cups cheese, grated
1 can green chilies, chopped

1/4 cup taco sauce
2 cooked chicken breasts,
   chopped

Mix together the soup, sour cream and chicken. Combine the cheese and chilies and set aside. Spoon chicken mixture into flour tortillas, add cheese mixture and taco sauce, to taste. Roll the filled tortillas and place in a 13x9x2-inch baking dish, split side down. Pour remaining mixture(s) over tortillas and bake at 350° for 30 minutes or until light brown. Makes 12 tortillas.

RUSSIAN CHICKEN

1 bottle Russian salad dressing   1 bottle teriyaki marinade
4 boneless chicken breasts

Marinate chicken breasts in the teriyaki marinade for several hours. Cut chicken into small pieces. Pour Russian dressing into large skillet and bring to a boil. Add chicken and cook on medium heat for 25 minutes until chicken becomes glazed. Stir frequently. Serve over rice. 4 servings.

MEXICAN CHICKEN CASSEROLE

1 chicken, boiled
1 can cream of chicken soup
1 can cream of mushroom
  soup
1 1/2 cups chicken broth
1/2 pound grated Cheddar
  cheese

1 (11 ounce) package nachos,
  crushed
1 can tomatoes and green
  chilies

Bone and cut chicken into bite-size pieces. Add undiluted soups, broth, tomatoes and green chilies and all but 1/4 of the cheese. Add crushed nachos and pour into a 13x9x2-inch casserole. Sprinkle remainder of cheese on top. Bake at 350° for about 20 minutes. 4 to 6 servings.

CHICKEN POT PIE

1 chicken, boiled
3 eggs, boiled
1 1/2 cups chicken broth
1 cup self-rising flour
1 stick margarine, melted

1 cup milk
1 can cream of chicken soup
1 can mixed vegetables
Salt and pepper, to taste

Debone and cut up chicken into bite-size pieces. Mix chicken, soup, broth, boiled eggs and canned vegetables in a large bowl. Pour into a 4 quart baking dish. Mix together flour, melted margarine and milk in a small bowl and pour over top of chicken mixture. Bake at 350° for 1 hour or until lightly brown. 4 to 6 servings.

CHICKEN CASSEROLE

2 cups chicken meat, chopped
1 cup (8 ounces) sour cream
1 can cream of chicken soup
1 stack of round butter
   flavored crackers

1 cup Cheddar cheese, grated
1 stick margarine

Mix together chicken, sour cream and soup. Pour into a 13x9x2-inch baking dish. Crumble crackers and Cheddar cheese on top of chicken mixture. Melt margarine and pour on top. Do not stir. Bake at 350° for 30 to 35 minutes. 4 servings.

SWEET AND SOUR CHICKEN

1 (15 ounce) can pineapple
   chunks in juice
2 chicken breasts, boneless and
   skinless
2 tablespoons oil
1/4 cup light corn syrup
1/4 cup red wine vinegar

2 tablespoons catsup
2 tablespoons soy sauce
1 tablespoon cornstarch
2 tablespoons water
1 green bell pepper, chopped
Hot rice

Drain pineapple, reserving juice; set aside. Cut chicken into 1 inch
pieces. Heat oil over medium heat. Add chicken and cook
approximately 5 to 10 minutes or until fork tender and cooked
thoroughly. Add the pineapple juice, corn syrup, red wine vinegar,
catsup and soy sauce; heat to boiling. Reduce heat to low and simmer 10
minutes, stirring occasionally. Combine cornstarch and water in a cup;
add to simmering chicken. Add bell pepper and pineapple. Stir until
thickened. Serve over rice. 2 servings.

CHICKEN-VEGETABLE CASSEROLE

1 chicken, boiled and cut up
1 can cream of chicken soup
1 can cream of celery soup
3 tablespoons salad dressing

2 tablespoons margarine
1 (2 pound) bag blended
  vegetables (broccoli, carrots
  and cauliflower)

Place chicken in bottom of a 13x9x2-inch casserole dish. Mix other ingredients together and pour over chicken. Cover and bake at 350° for 1 hour. 8 servings.

BACON-WRAPPED CHICKEN-MUSHROOM KABOBS

2 large chicken breast filets
10 large mushrooms
1/4 cup soy sauce
1/4 cup cider vinegar
2 tablespoons honey
2 tablespoons salad oil

2 small green onions, minced
1 (8 ounce) can pineapple
  chunks
1 (8 ounce) package sliced
  bacon

Cut each chicken breast in half; then cut each breast half into 5 chunks.
Cut each mushroom in half. In a large bowl, mix mushrooms halves,
chicken pieces, soy sauce, cider vinegar, honey, salad oil, green onions
and juice from pineapple. Let this marinate while preparing remaining
ingredients. Prepare outdoor grill for barbecuing. Cut each bacon slice
crosswise in half. Wrap each bacon piece around a piece of chicken and
a mushroom half. On 4 long skewers, thread bacon-wrapped chicken
and pineapple pieces. Reserve soy-sauce mixture to brush on chicken
kabobs. Cook about 15 to 20 minutes on grill or until chicken is fork-
tender and bacon is crisp. 4 servings.

CREAMY CHICKEN BREASTS

4 chicken breasts
8 slices Swiss cheese
1 can cream of chicken soup
1/4 cup sour cream

1 cup herb seasoned stuffing
    mix, crushed
1/4 cup margarine, melted

Split, skin and debone chicken breast. Arrange in a greased 13x9-inch baking dish. Top with cheese slices. Combine soup and sour cream; stir and spoon evenly over chicken. Sprinkle with stuffing mix. Drizzle margarine over crumbs. Bake at 350° for 45 minutes. 4 servings.

SWEET AND SOUR PORK

6 pork chops
2 tablespoons margarine
2 green peppers, chopped
2 onions, chopped
1 (13 1/2 ounce) can pineapple
    chunks

1 tablespoon vinegar
2 tablespoons brown sugar
2 teaspoons cornstarch
1/3 cup water
Salt and pepper to taste

Cut meat from bones and cut into 1-inch pieces. In a skillet, brown pork in margarine. Add chopped onion and pepper and sauté until clear. Add pineapple juice. Cook over low heat for 10 minutes. Add pineapple chunks, salt, pepper, brown sugar, vinegar and a small amount of water. Cook 10 minutes longer. Mix cornstarch with 1/3 cup water and add to pork mixture. Simmer for 5 minutes. Serve over rice. 6 servings.

SAUCY PORK CHOPS

4 to 6 pork chops	3 tablespoons margarine
1 small can mandarin oranges	1 teaspoon mustard
(reserve juice)	$1/3$ cup brown sugar

Mix together margarine, mustard, juice and sugar; pour into a greased casserole dish. Add the pork chops and pour mandarin oranges on top. Brown in a 375° oven , turning once during baking. 4 to 6 servings.

PORK CHOPS AND SCALLOPED POTATOES

4 pork chops
2 tablespoons all-purpose
   flour
1/8 teaspoon black pepper

2 teaspoons salt
1 tablespoon margarine
4 cups potatoes, thinly sliced
2 cups milk

Season and brown pork chops. Combine flour, salt and pepper. Alternate layers of potatoes and flour mixture in a buttered 1 1/2 quart baking dish. Dot with margarine. Pour milk over all. Top with pork chops. Cover and bake at 375° for 45 minutes. Remove cover and bake about 15 minutes longer or until potatoes are browned. 4 servings.

HAM AND BROCCOLI BAKE

2 cups ham, diced
2 cups broccoli, chopped
1 medium onion, chopped
3 slices bread
1 1/2 cups Cheddar cheese,
    shredded

3 eggs
1/2 teaspoon mustard
1 1/2 cups milk

Arrange bread in greased, shallow 1 1/2 quart baking dish. In a large bowl, combine ham, broccoli, onion and 1 cup of the cheese. Beat eggs lightly with mustard. Add to ham mixture and pour in milk. Spread on top of bread and sprinkle with remaining cheese. Bake at 350° for 1 hour or until well browned. 4 to 6 servings.

HAM AND POTATO CASSEROLE

1 can cream of mushroom
   soup
4 cups potatoes, sliced
3/4 cup milk

1 cup ham, diced
1 small onion, sliced
1 tablespoon margarine
Salt and pepper, to taste

Blend soup, milk, salt and pepper. In a 1½ quart casserole dish, alternate layers of ham, potatoes and onion. Dot top with margarine. Pour soup mixture over top and bake at 375° for 30 minutes. Uncover and bake 15 minutes longer or until potatoes are tender. 4 servings.

MEAT LOAF

11/2 pounds ground beef
2 eggs, beaten
3/4 cup milk
1/2 cup bread crumbs
1/4 cup onion, chopped
1/2 teaspoon salt

1/2 teaspoon ground sage
1 teaspoon dry mustard
1/8 teaspoon pepper
1/4 cup ketchup
2 tablespoons brown sugar

In a medium bowl combine eggs, milk, bread crumbs, onion, salt, sage and pepper. Add ground beef. Thoroughly mix meat and seasonings. Place in a 8x4-inch loaf pan and pat down. Bake at 350° for 1 hour. Mix together ketchup, brown sugar and dry mustard and spread over top of meat loaf. Bake 10 minutes longer. 6 servings.

SWISS PIE

1 cup round butter flavored
   crackers (about 28), crushed
1/4 cup margarine, melted
6 slices bacon
1 cup onion, chopped
2 cups (8 ounces) Swiss cheese,
   shredded

2 eggs, slightly beaten
3/4 cup sour cream
1/2 teaspoon salt
1/2 cup sharp Cheddar cheese,
   shredded

Combine cracker crumbs and margarine; press into bottom and sides of an 8-inch pie plate. Cook bacon until crisp; drain; crumble; set aside. Pour off all but 2 tablespoons of bacon fat. Add onion and cook until tender but not brown. Combine crumbled bacon, onion, Swiss cheese, eggs, sour cream, salt and a dash of pepper in a medium bowl and mix well. Sprinkle Cheddar cheese on top. Bake at 375° for 25 to 30 minutes, or until knife inserted in center comes out clean. Let stand 5 to 10 minutes before cutting. 4 to 6 servings.

QUICHE

3 slices bacon
1 cup sour cream
1/2 cup mushrooms, chopped
1/2 teaspoon Worcestershire
  sauce
1 (31/2 ounce) can French fried
  onion rings, chopped

3 eggs, beaten
3/4 teaspoon salt
1 (9-inch) baked pastry shell
1 cup Swiss cheese, grated

Preheat oven to 325°. Fry, drain and crumble bacon. Combine eggs, sour cream, salt and Worcestershire sauce. Stir in bacon, onion rings and cheese. Pour into baked pie shell. Bake 45 to 50 minutes or until custard is set and brown on top. May be partially cooled 30 minutes and frozen. 4 to 6 servings.

GREAT STEAKS

4 T-bone steaks
2 teaspoons brown sugar
2 small green onions, minced

1 teaspoon ginger
1 clove garlic, minced
1/4 cup soy sauce

Mix sugar, garlic, onion, ginger and soy sauce together. Place steaks in pan and pour sauce over them. Let stand in refrigerator for 2 hours, turning once. Prepare grill for barbecuing or broil in oven. Brush sauce on steaks while cooking. 4 servings.

EASY LASAGNA CASSEROLE

3 cups uncooked egg noodles
1 pound ground beef
1/2 cup onion, chopped
1 (3 ounce) package cream
   cheese
1 cup evaporated milk

1 (15 ounce) can tomato sauce
1 (15 ounce) package spaghetti
   sauce mix
1/2 teaspoon garlic salt
1 cup mozzarella cheese,
   shredded

Boil noodles until tender; drain. Cook ground beef and onion in skillet until browned. Drain fat. Stir in tomato sauce and spaghetti sauce mix. Cook until thickened. Combine cream cheese and evaporated milk in saucepan and cook on low heat until mixture is smooth. Stir in noodles and garlic salt. Pour mixture into a greased 9-inch square baking dish. Spread on meat mixture. Top with mozzarella cheese. Bake at 350° for 20 minutes or until bubbly. 6 servings.

BEEF STIR-FRY

3 to 4 ounces lean beef, cut in
    strips
1 teaspoon margarine
1/2 cup onion, chopped
1/2 cup green pepper, cut in
    strips

1/2 cup celery, cut in strips
1/2 cup cooked leftover
    vegetables
3 cups cooked rice
Soy sauce to taste
Salt and pepper to taste

Melt margarine over medium high heat. Stir-fry meat and onions for 3
minutes. Add celery and peppers; stir-fry for 1 minute. Add cooked rice
and leftover vegetables. Stir until hot. Add soy sauce and salt and
pepper to taste. 2 to 3 servings.

TACO CASSEROLE

1 to 2 pounds ground beef
1 can cream of mushroom soup
1 or 2 cans diced tomatoes with
    green chilies
1 package taco seasoning mix

1 onion, chopped
1 small package pasteurized
    process cheese spread
1 can cream of chicken soup
1 package corn chips

In a large skillet brown beef and onions together and drain. Add taco seasoning and cook as directed on package. Stir in soups and tomatoes. Crush chips and layer in bottom of greased 13x9x2-inch casserole dish. Top with beef mixture, then cheese. Pour 1/2 of the soup mixture over cheese. Repeat layers. Bake at 400° for 20 minutes or until bubbly. 4 to 6 servings.

MEXICAN CASSEROLE

2 pounds ground chuck
1 large onion, chopped
1 can cream of chicken soup
1 can mild enchilada sauce
1 dozen tortilla shells

1 can tomatoes with green
  chilies
10 to 12 ounces Cheddar
  cheese, grated

Combine tomatoes, soup and enchilada sauce in saucepan over medium heat until well blended. Brown ground chuck and drain off excess fat; salt to taste. In large casserole dish, place layers of tortilla shells, meat, onion and cheese and pour sauce over top. Repeat until all ingredients are used, ending with layer of cheese and remaining sauce. Bake at 350° for approximately 1 hour, or until brown on top. 4 to 6 servings.

SPOONBURGERS

3 tablespoons margarine
1 1/2 pounds ground meat
2 large onions, chopped
3 green peppers, chopped
3 tomatoes, peeled and
  chopped

3 teaspoons chili powder
1/4 teaspoon pepper
1 cup ketchup
6 buns

Mix all ingredients together in a large skillet except ketchup and cook for about 10 minutes until light brown. Add ketchup and simmer 20 to 30 minutes. Serve on toasted buns. 6 servings.

HAMBURGER HASH

2 pounds ground beef
1 bell pepper, chopped
1 onion, diced
1 teaspoon chili powder

1 1/2 cups dry rice
2 can tomatoes
Salt and pepper to taste

Brown ground beef, onions and bell pepper; add salt, pepper and chili powder. Simmer a few minutes and add dry rice and tomatoes. Cool until rice is done over low heat. 4 to 6 servings.

SALMON PATTIES

1 can salmon	2 tablespoons parsley
1/2 cup margarine	1 medium onion
2 eggs	1 cup dry bread crumbs

Remove any bones from salmon; add eggs, parsley, onion and bread crumbs. Mix well and shape into patties. Coat in flour; fry in melted margarine until brown on both sides. 4 servings.

SHRIMP CASSEROLE

2 cans shrimp, drained
3/4 cup milk
1 cup mild Cheddar cheese,
   grated
1/4 teaspoon black pepper

2 cups saltine crackers, broken
1 teaspoon Worcestershire
   sauce
3 eggs, beaten

Mix beaten eggs, milk, black pepper and Worcestershire. In a 2 quart casserole layer 1/2 cup crackers, 1/3 cup cheese, 1/3 cup of shrimp. Pour 1/3 cup of milk mixture over layer and repeat layers ending with crackers. Bake at 350° for 45 minutes or until set. 4 servings.

NOTES

Desserts

CHOCOLATE POUND CAKE

1 cup margarine
1/2 cup shortening
3 cups sugar
5 eggs
3 cups all-purpose flour

1/4 teaspoon salt
2/3 teaspoon baking powder
1/2 cup cocoa
1 teaspoon vanilla extract
11/4 cups milk

Sift dry ingredients. Cream together margarine, shortening and sugar. Beat in eggs. Add dry ingredients alternating with milk. Pour into greased and floured tube pan and bake in preheated oven at 300° for 11/2 hours.

LEMON POUND CAKE

1 cup margarine
1/2 cup shortening
3 cups sugar
6 eggs
1/2 teaspoon baking powder

1/4 teaspoon salt
3 cups all-purpose flour
1 cup milk
2 teaspoons lemon extract

In a mixing bowl cream together margarine and shortening. Gradually add sugar, creaming well. Add the eggs, one at a time, beating well after each addition. Sift together dry ingredients and add to creamed mixture alternately with milk and continue beating. Add flavoring and pour into greased and floured tube pan. Bake at 325° for 1 1/4 hours or until toothpick comes out clean.

CHOCOLATE BUNDT CAKE

1 box butter cake mix
1 small box milk chocolate
   instant pudding
1 cup sour cream
1/2 cup salad oil

1/4 cup water
4 eggs
1 cup chocolate chips
1/2 cup chopped nuts

Mix all ingredients together and bake in greased and floured bundt pan for 1 hour at 350°.

GLAZE:
3 tablespoons margarine
2 tablespoons cocoa

1 tablespoon milk
2/3 cup powdered sugar

Melt margarine in small saucepan. Add cocoa, milk and bring to boil. Remove and add powdered sugar. Stir and pour over warm cake.

DREAM CAKE

1 angel food cake (broken into
    pieces)
2 packages whipped topping
1 cup cold milk

1 cup confectioners sugar
1 (8 ounce) package cream
    cheese
1 can cherry pie filling

Beat whipped topping and milk together. Add sugar and mix well. Beat
cream cheese until smooth. Add whipped topping to cream cheese a
little at a time. Place a layer of cake pieces in 13x9-inch pan, then a layer
of whipped topping. Alternate layers. Pour cherry pie filling on top and
chill overnight. 12 servings.

PRUNE CAKE

2 cups sugar
1 cup oil
3 eggs
2 jars baby food prunes with
    tapioca
2 cups self-rising flour

1 teaspoon each of cloves,
    allspice, cinnamon, nutmeg
1 cup nuts
1 teaspoon vanilla extract
Pinch salt

Mix first 4 ingredients with mixer. Add flour and spices. Beat at high speed for 5 minutes. Add nuts (rolled in flour before adding to batter). Mix in vanilla and salt. Bake at 350° for about 1 1/2 hours.

STRAWBERRY CAKE

1 box yellow cake mix	2/3 cup oil
1 box strawberry Jello	4 eggs
2 tablespoons sugar	1/2 cup water
1/2 cup strawberries	

Mix all the ingredients in a large bowl. Bake at 350° until toothpick comes out clean (about 20 to 25 minutes). Makes 3 layers.

ICING:

1 box powdered sugar	1/2 cup strawberries
3 tablespoons margarine	

Beat with mixer until smooth and ice the cooled cake.

ORANGE-COCONUT CAKE

1 orange cake mix
1 can cream of coconut
1 can sweetened condensed
    milk
1 (16 ounce) whipped topping

2 (6 ounce) packages fresh
    frozen coconut
1 (7 ounce) package flaked
    coconut

Mix and bake cake mix according to directions on package. While cake is hot mix together cream of coconut and milk. Pour over cake. Cool. Mix together whipped topping and coconuts. Top cake with this mixture and refrigerate before serving.

3-DAY EASY COCONUT CAKE

1 white cake mix
2 packages frozen coconut
1 (8 ounce) sour cream

1 cup sugar
1 (8 ounce) whipped topping

Mix cake according to directions on box. Split into 4 layers. Mix 1 1/2 packages of coconut with sour cream and sugar. Set aside 1/2 cup of mixture for later use. Spread the rest between layers. Mix the 1/2 cup mixture with whipped topping and spread on top and sides. Sprinkle rest of coconut on top of cake. Refrigerate for 3 days in an airtight container before cutting.

BANANA SPLIT CAKE

2 cups graham cracker crumbs
1 large can crushed pineapple,
    drained
1 box powdered sugar
1 cup margarine, softened

1/2 cup margarine, melted
2 teaspoons sugar
5 bananas, sliced
1 (12 ounce) whipped topping
1/2 cut nuts, chopped

Combine cracker crumbs, melted margarine and sugar and mix well. Pat into 13x9-inch pan. Bake at 300° for 10 minutes. Cool. Mix powdered sugar and softened margarine until light and fluffy. Pour over crust. Spread pineapple over top, followed by whipped topping. Sprinkle with nuts. Chill thoroughly. A layer of strawberries may also be placed over bananas for a variation. 12 to 14 servings.

EARTHQUAKE CAKE

1 German chocolate cake mix
1 cup pecans, chopped
1 cup coconut
1 (8 ounce) package cream
    cheese

1 box powdered sugar
1 teaspoon vanilla extract

In a greased 9x13-inch pan place the pecans and coconut. Mix cake mix according to directions on box and pour over the pecans and coconut. Do not stir. In a separate bowl mix together the cream cheese, powdered sugar and vanilla. Beat until creamy and drop by spoonfuls over cake mix. Bake at 350° for 30 to 35 minutes. Serve with whipped topping. 12 to 14 servings.

CHOCOLATE SHEET CAKE

2 cups sugar
2 cups all-purpose flour
1 stick margarine
4 tablespoons cocoa
1/2 cup shortening
1 cup water

1/2 cup buttermilk
1 teaspoon vanilla extract
2 eggs, slightly beaten
1 teaspoon soda
1 teaspoon cinnamon

Sift together in a large bowl the sugar and flour. In a sauce pan, bring to a rapid boil the margarine, cocoa, shortening and water. Pour over flour mixture and stir well. Then add the buttermilk, vanilla, soda, cinnamon and eggs. Bake in a greased 13x9-inch pan for 20 to 25 minutes at 350°.

ICING - PREPARE 5 MINUTES BEFORE CAKE IS DONE:
1/4 cup margarine
3 tablespoons evaporated milk

2 tablespoons cocoa

(continued to next page)

Cook these on medium heat until melted. Then stir in the following and mix well.

1/2 box confectioners sugar   1/2 cup pecans
1 teaspoon vanilla extract

Spread over hot cake. 12 to 14 servings.

PINEAPPLE CAKE

1 cake mix   1 large can crushed pineapple
1 can sweetened condensed   1 large container whipped
   milk   topping

Mix cake mix according to directions on box. Bake in a greased and floured 9x13-inch pan. Remove cake from oven and while warm, pour condensed milk over cake. Then spread on the crushed pineapple, top with whipped topping. Refrigerate or freeze until needed. 12 to 14 servings.

APRICOT CAKE

1 box yellow or lemon cake mix	1 cup apricot or pear nectar
2/3 cup oil	1 cup confectioners sugar
4 eggs	Juice from 1 lemon

Mix cake mix according to directions on box. Add apricot or pear nectar. Bake in a greased tube pan at 350° for 45 minutes. Combine confectioners sugar and lemon juice. Glaze top of cake and let drip down the sides.

FRESH APPLE CAKE

2 cups sugar	3 eggs
3 cups all-purpose flour	1 teaspoon vanilla extract
1 teaspoon soda	3/4 cup vegetable oil
1 teaspoon salt	3 cups apples, chopped
1 teaspoon cinnamon	1 cup pecans, chopped
1/2 cup applesauce	

Mix together dry ingredients. Add applesauce, oil, eggs and vanilla. Stir in nuts and apples. Bake at 350° for 1 hour in a greased tube pan.

CARROT CAKE AND FROSTING

2 cups all-purpose flour
1 teaspoon salt
2 teaspoons baking soda
2 cups sugar
2 teaspoons cinnamon
2 teaspoons vanilla extract
1 1/2 cups oil
4 eggs

2 cups carrots, grated
1 cup crushed pineapple
1/2 cups nuts, chopped
1 box confectioners sugar
1/2 stick margarine
1 (8 ounce) package cream
   cheese, softened
2 teaspoons vanilla extract

Combine flour, salt, sugar, soda and cinnamon together. Add vanilla; stir in oil, beat well. Add eggs, one at a time, beating after each one. Add carrots, pineapple and nuts. Stir to blend. Pour into a 13x9-inch pan and bake at 350° for 50 minutes. Cool.

FROSTING: Beat cream cheese, confectioners sugar and margarine; add vanilla. Frost.

APPLESAUCE-CHOCOLATE CHIP CAKE

2 cups all-purpose flour
1 1/2 teaspoons salt
1 1/2 teaspoons soda
1/2 teaspoon nutmeg
1/2 teaspoon allspice
1/2 cup shortening
2 cups applesauce
2 cups raisins

2 tablespoons cocoa
1/2 teaspoon cinnamon
2 eggs
1 1/2 cups sugar
1 cup pecans
2 tablespoons sugar
1 (6 ounce) package chocolate
chips

Combine flour, salt, soda, spices, cocoa and sugar in a large mixing bowl. Add shortening, eggs and applesauce and beat well. Stir in 1/2 cups pecans and raisins. Pour into a greased and floured 10x13-inch cake pan. Sprinkle with remaining 1/2 cup of pecans and chocolate chips. Sprinkle with 2 tablespoons sugar. Bake at 350° for 40 minutes. 8 to 10 servings.

CHOCOLATE PUDDING CAKE

1 cup self-rising flour
3/4 cup sugar
2 tablespoons cocoa
1/2 cup milk
3 tablespoons margarine,
   melted

1/2 cup packed brown sugar
1 teaspoon vanilla extract
1/2 cup sugar
1/4 cup cocoa
11/2 cups water

Sift together 3/4 cup sugar, flour and 2 tablespoons cocoa into a 9-inch square pan. Stir in milk, margarine and vanilla and spread mixture evenly into pan. Combine brown sugar, 1/2 cup sugar and 1/4 cup cocoa and sprinkle over batter. Pour water on top. Do not stir. Bake at 350° for 40 minutes. Serve with ice cream. 4 to 6 servings.

CHOCOLATE BROWNIE CAKE

3 cups all-purpose flour	5 eggs
1/2 teaspoon salt	1/2 cup cocoa
2 sticks margarine	1 cup milk
1/2 cup shortening	2 teaspoons vanilla extract
3 cups sugar	

Cream margarine, shortening and sugar in mixing bowl until well blended. Add eggs and vanilla. Sift dry ingredients and add alternately with milk to the mixture. Bake in a tube pan at 325° for 1 hour 25 minutes.

SEVEN-UP CAKE

1 box yellow or lemon cake
  mix
4 eggs
1 package instant vanilla
  pudding

2/3 cup oil
1 1/2 cups 7-Up

Mix cake mix, eggs, pudding and oil together and beat for 3 minutes until light and fluffy. Add 7-Up and beat for another minute. Pour into greased and floured 9x13-inch pan. Bake at 350° for 40 minutes.

ICING:
1 1/2 cups sugar
1 tablespoon flour
2 eggs, beaten
1/2 cup margarine, melted

1 cup crushed pineapple and
  juice
1 1/2 cups coconut

In a large saucepan cook until thick the sugar, flour, eggs, margarine and pineapple and juice. Stir in coconut and pour over hot cake.

EASY CHEESECAKE

BLEND TOGETHER AND PRESS INTO 9X13-INCH PAN:

1 box yellow cake mix	1 egg
1 stick margarine	

MIX:

1 (8 ounce) package cream cheese	2 eggs
	1 teaspoon vanilla extract
1 box confectioners sugar	

Beat 3 to 4 minutes. Pour on cake mixture and bake for 30 minutes at 350°. 10 to 12 servings.

ICE CREAM ROLL CAKE

1 box cake mix (any flavor)   **1/2 gallon ice cream (any flavor)**

Mix cake mix according to directions on box. Pour into a greased and floured cookie sheet with sides and bake for 15 minutes at 350° or until toothpick comes out clean. Cool. Cut 2 strips of butcher paper or foil about 25 inches long and overlap. Turn cake over onto the paper or foil. Soften ice cream at room temperature until spreadable. Using a spatula, spread ice cream over cake evenly. Roll cake in a jelly roll fashion. It will break all to pieces, but it will freeze solid. Pull paper tight and tape. Place in freezer. Needs to be made the day before it is served. 10 to 12 servings.

VANILLA WAFER CAKE

2 cups sugar
2 sticks margarine
6 eggs, slightly beaten
1 (12 ounce) box vanilla
   wafers, crushed

1 cup pecans, chopped
1 (3 1/2 ounce) can flaked
   coconut

Cream together sugar and margarine. Add eggs, crushed vanilla wafers, pecans and coconut. Mix well. Batter will be stiff. Spread in a greased and floured 10-inch tube pan and bake for 1 1/2 hours at 325°.

TURTLE CAKE

1 box German chocolate cake mix	1 large package chocolate morsels
1 large bag caramels	1 cup chopped pecans
1 large can evaporated milk	

Mix batter; pour 1/2 mix into a greased and floured 13x9x2-inch dish and cook for 20 minutes at 350°. Melt caramels and evaporated milk together and pour over cooled cake. Put chocolate morsels and pecans on top of this mixture. Pour remainder of cake batter on top and cook another 20 minutes.

FLAKY PIE CRUST

2 cups all-purpose flour
1 cup shortening

1/2 teaspoon salt
1/4 cup ice water

Mix flour and salt together in a bowl. Cut shortening into flour until mixture resembles coarse meal. Sprinkle with water, a little at a time, mixing quickly with a fork after each spoonful. Add only enough water so dough holds together and can be formed into a ball. Divide dough into two balls handling as little as possible. Roll dough out onto a floured surface. Yields: 2 9-inch pie crusts.

GRAHAM CRACKER CRUST

18 graham cracker squares   **6 tablespoons margarine**
1/4 cup sugar

Place graham crackers in a plastic bag and crush into fine crumbs with dough roller. Measure 1 1/4 cups of crumbs. Place crumbs in a medium bowl and stir in sugar. Melt margarine and add to crumb mixture. Mix well. Pour crumb mixture into a 9-inch pie plate and pat onto sides and bottom. Chill for 1 hour or bake in a 375° oven for 6 minutes or until brown. Cool before filling. Yields: 1 9-inch pie crust.

NO WORRY MERINGUE

1 tablespoon cornstarch
1/2 teaspoon cold water
1/2 cup boiling water

3 egg whites
6 tablespoons sugar
1 teaspoon vanilla extract

Mix cornstarch with cold water in a saucepan. Add boiling water and cook until thick, stirring constantly. Remove from heat and cool. Beat egg whites to soft peaks. Add cooled corn starch mixture and beat until well mixed and stiff. Add vanilla and mix well. Spoon on pie and seal edges. Bake at 350° for 15 minutes.

EASY MERINGUE

3 egg whites
Dash of salt

1 cup marshmallow cream

Beat 1 cup marshmallow cream until fluffy. In a separate bowl, beat egg whites and salt until soft peak forms. Gradually add marshmallow cream, beating until stiff peaks form. Spread over pie filling, sealing to edge of crust. Bake at 350° for 12 to 15 minutes or until lightly browned. Yields: 1 meringue.

118 Desserts

APPLE PIE

6 cups tart apples, sliced thin
3/4 cup sugar
1/4 cup brown sugar
2 tablespoons flour
1/2 teaspoon cinnamon

1/4 teaspoon ground nutmeg
1/8 teaspoon salt
1/4 cup heavy cream
3 tablespoons margarine
Pastry for double pie crust

Line a pie pan with half of the pastry. Add 1/3 apples. Mix sugar, flour, cinnamon, nutmeg and salt together. Sprinkle 1/3 over apples. Repeat layers. Pour cream into center of pie. Dot with margarine. Cover with top crust and slit the dough. Brush with milk and sprinkle with sugar. Bake at 400° for 1 hour.

ENGLISH APPLE PIE

4 apples, peeled and sliced
1 cup sugar
1 teaspoon cinnamon
1/2 cup margarine

1/2 cup brown sugar
1/2 cup pecans, chopped
1 teaspoon cinnamon
1 cup all-purpose flour

Butter large baking dish. Place apples in bottom of dish and sprinkle 1 cup sugar and 1 teaspoon cinnamon over them. Cream margarine and brown sugar together and add cinnamon, flour and pecans. Spread over apples. Bake at 350° for 1 hour. Cool and serve with ice cream. 4 to 6 servings.

APPLE DUMP PIE

1 can sliced apples
1 box yellow or butter pecan
   cake mix

1 teaspoon cinnamon
2 sticks margarine
1/2 cup brown sugar

Pour apples in a 9x5-inch baking dish. Sprinkle with brown sugar and cinnamon and cover with dry cake mix. Cut sticks of margarine into thin slices and cover mixture. Bake at 300° for 1 hour. Serve warm with ice cream. 4 to 6 servings.

COCONUT PIE

1 (7 ounce) can coconut
3 eggs, beaten
1 1/2 cups sugar
2 tablespoons flour

1 stick margarine, melted
1 teaspoon vanilla extract
3/4 cup buttermilk
9-inch unbaked pie crust

Mix all the ingredients together and pour into an unbaked pie crust. Bake for 1 hour at 325°.

CRUSTY COCONUT PIE

1/2 cup milk
11/4 cups coconut
1/4 cup margarine

1 cup sugar
3 eggs
1 teaspoon vanilla extract
9-inch unbaked pie crust

Pour milk over coconut and set aside. Cream margarine and sugar. Add eggs and beat well. Then add milk , coconut and vanilla. Pour into an unbaked pie crust. Bake at 350° for 30 minutes or until pie is golden brown and firm.

FUDGE PIE

1/2 stick margarine, melted
3 tablespoons cocoa
11/2 cups sugar
2 eggs

1/2 cup evaporated milk
1 teaspoon vanilla extract
9-inch unbaked pie crust

Mix well and pour into an unbaked pie crust and bake at 400° for 10 minutes, then turn oven down to 350° and bake for an additional 20 minutes.

122 Desserts

QUICK CHOCOLATE PIE

1 deep dish graham cracker   6 chocolate bars with almonds
  crust   1 (12 ounce) whipped topping

In a double boiler, bring water to a boil and turn off. Place candy bars in boiler and melt. Mix immediately with whipped topping and pour into pie crust. Chill.

CHOCOLATE CHIP PIE

1 cup sugar   1 cup nuts, chopped
1/2 cup all-purpose flour   1 cup chocolate chips
2 eggs, slightly beaten   1 teaspoon vanilla extract
1 stick margarine, melted and   9-inch unbaked pie crust
  cooled

Mix together sugar and flour. Add remaining ingredients; mix. Pour into pie crust. Bake at 325° for 1 hour. Serve hot or cold.

CHOCOLATE PIE

4 egg yolks
2 tablespoons flour
2 tablespoons cocoa
2 cups sugar

2 cups milk
2 tablespoons margarine
9-inch unbaked pie crust

Mix ingredients in order listed. Cook until thick in large skillet. Pour mixture into pie crust. Bake at 325° until crust is brown.

MERINGUE:
4 egg whites   3 tablespoons sugar

Beat eggs and sugar together until very thick. Pour on pie. Return to oven to brown meringue.

CHOCOLATE CHESS PIE

2 eggs, beaten
1 stick margarine, melted
1 small can evaporated milk
1 teaspoon vanilla extract

1 1/2 cups sugar
3 1/2 tablespoons cocoa
9-inch unbaked pie crust

Mix well and pour into pie crust. Bake 45 minutes at 325°.

CHESS PIE

6 eggs
3 cups sugar
2 sticks margarine

3 tablespoons vinegar
1 teaspoon vanilla extract
2 unbaked pie shells

Melt margarine, add sugar and eggs; mix well. Add remaining
ingredients and pour into unbaked pie shells. Bake at 275° until firm.
Makes 2 pies.

COCONUT-CARAMEL PIE

1/4 cup margarine
1/2 cup pecans, chopped
1 (7 ounce) package flaked
   coconut
1 (8 ounce) package cream
   cheese, softened

1 (14 ounce) can sweetened
   condensed milk
1 (16 ounce) whipped
   topping
1 (12 ounce) jar caramel ice
   cream topping

Prepare recipe for crust below. While the crust is baking, melt margarine
in skillet. Add coconut and pecans. Cook until golden brown. Set aside.
Combine cream cheese and condensed milk and beat until smooth. Fold
in whipped topping. Layer 1/2 of cream cheese mixture over crust.
Sprinkle 1/2 of coconut mixture over cream cheese mixture. Then drizzle
half of the caramel topping over the coconut mixture. Repeat layers.
Cover and freeze until firm.

CRUST:
1/2 cup brown sugar   1/2 stick margarine, melted
1 cup self-rising flour

(continued to next page)

Mix all ingredients together and press in a 9x13-inch pan (that can be placed in freezer later). Bake at 350° for 15 minutes. Cool and take a fork and crumble crust. 10 to 12 servings.

FRESH BLUEBERRY PIE

2 1/2 cups fresh blueberries
1 cup sour cream
3/4 cup sugar
1 egg, beaten
2 tablespoons all-purpose
   flour
1 teaspoon vanilla extract
1/4 teaspoon salt
3 tablespoons all-purpose
   flour
2 tablespoons margarine
3 tablespoons nuts, chopped
9-inch unbaked pie crust

Mix together sour cream, 2 tablespoons flour, sugar, vanilla, salt and egg. Beat until smooth. Fold in blueberries. Pour filling into unbaked pie crust. Bake at 400° for 25 minutes. In a small bowl, combine flour, margarine and nuts and sprinkle over top of pie. Bake an additional 10 minutes.

OUTRAGEOUS PIE

11/4 cups sugar
11/2 cups graham cracker
  crumbs, crushed
11/2 cups pecans
11/2 cups coconut

7 egg whites
9-inch unbaked pie crust
Bananas
Whipped topping

Mix sugar, crumbs, pecans, coconut and egg whites together; stir by hand. Pour into an unbaked pie crust. Bake at 325° for 25 to 30 minutes or until glossy and set. Do not overbake. Serve warm with sliced bananas and whipped topping.

JAPANESE FRUIT PIE

2 cups sugar
1 cup nuts, chopped
4 eggs, beaten
2 teaspoons vanilla extract

2 sticks margarine, melted
1 cup raisins
1 cup coconut
2 unbaked pie shells

Mix all ingredients together except eggs, beat in one at a time. Pour into unbaked pie shells and bake at 350° for 40 to 45 minutes. Makes 2 pies.

LEMON CHESS PIE

11/2 cups sugar
1 tablespoon flour
1 tablespoon meal
4 eggs
1/4 cup margarine, melted

1/4 cup milk
2 tablespoons lemon juice
1/4 teaspoon lemon flavoring
9-inch pie crust

In a large bowl, toss lightly the flour, sugar and meal with a fork. Add eggs, melted margarine, milk, lemon juice and lemon flavoring. Beat with a mixer until smooth and blended. Pour filling into pie crust. Bake at 375° until golden brown.

EASY LEMON PIE

1 small can frozen lemonade
   concentrate
1 can sweetened condensed milk

1 large whipped topping
1 graham cracker crust
Canned pie filling (if desired)

Mix whipped topping, lemonade and condensed milk until creamy. Pour into pie crust and refrigerate. Top with canned pie filling, if desired.

ORANGE JUICE PIE

1 (6 ounce) can frozen orange
   juice
1 package orange Jello
1 pint vanilla ice cream

1 can coconut
1 can mandarin oranges, diced
Whipped cream
9-inch baked pie crust

Mix orange juice with water to make 1 1/2 cups. Heat to boiling and dissolve the Jello in the juice. Let cool. Add the ice cream, coconut and mandarin oranges. Pour into a baked pie crust and chill. Top with whipped cream and garnish with orange slices, if desired.

PINEAPPLE PIE

1 can sweetened condensed milk
1 large can crushed pineapple,
   drained

1/4 cup lemon juice
1 (9 ounce) whipped topping
2 graham cracker crusts

Mix all ingredients together and pour into pie shells and chill for about 30 minutes. Make 2 pies.

PECAN PIE

3 egg whites
1 cup sugar
1/2 teaspoon baking powder
1 teaspoon vanilla extract

2/3 cup graham cracker
   crumbs
1 cup pecans, chopped
Whipped topping

Beat egg whites until stiff. Add baking powder. Gradually add sugar. Fold in graham cracker crumbs and pecans. Add vanilla and mix well. Bake in a greased glass pie plate for 30 minutes at 350°. Top with whipped topping. This pie makes it's own crust.

PECAN PIE

1/2 cup sugar
2 eggs, beaten
2 tablespoons all-purpose
   flour
1 1/2 tablespoons margarine,
   melted

1 cup light corn syrup
1 teaspoon vanilla extract
1/4 teaspoon salt
1 cup pecans, chopped
9-inch unbaked pie crust

Combine flour to sugar. Add to beaten eggs. Add other ingredients. Beat well. Stir in pecans. Pour into unbaked pie crust. Bake at 450° for 10 minutes. Reduce to 350° for 25 minutes.

HONEY PECAN PIE

1/2 cup honey
3 eggs
1/3 cup sugar
1/3 cup brown sugar
1/4 teaspoon salt

1/4 cup margarine, melted
1/2 cup white corn syrup
1 teaspoon vanilla extract
1 cup pecan halves
9-inch unbaked pie crust

Beat eggs, mix all other ingredients except pecans halves. Pour mixture into pie crust and place pecan halves on top. Bake at 375° for 40 to 50 minutes.

FRESH STRAWBERRY PIE

1 cup sugar
1 cup water
8 teaspoons cornstarch
Pinch of salt

4 tablespoons strawberry Jello
1 pint fresh strawberries
9-inch baked pie crust

Combine first 4 ingredients in large boiler. Boil until thick and clear. Add Jello, let cool. Add strawberries and pour into baked pie crust. Chill until firm. Top with whipped cream, when ready to serve.

PEANUT BUTTER PIE

1 small box vanilla pudding
   mix (not instant)
3/4 cup crunchy peanut butter
1 cup powdered sugar

1 graham cracker pie crust
1 package whipped topping
   mix

Mix pudding according to directions on box. In a separate bowl mix
together peanut butter and powdered sugar until crumbly with hands.
Place 1/2 of the peanut butter mixture in bottom of pie crust, then pour
warm pudding into crust. Put more peanut butter mixture on top of the
pudding, reserving some of the mixture to sprinkle on top of pie. Whip
the whip topping according to directions on box and place on top.
Sprinkle remaining peanut butter mixture on top of pie. Refrigerate
overnight before serving.

QUICK BANANA PUDDING

1 large package instant vanilla
   pudding
1 can sweetened condensed milk

1 large container whipped topping
1 box vanilla wafers
3 to 4 bananas

Mix instant pudding as directed on box. Stir in remaining ingredients.
Layer in a glass dish: bananas, vanilla wafers and pudding mixture until
gone. Garnish with wafers. 6 to 8 servings.

QUICK CHERRY DESSERT

1 can cherry pie filling
1/2 cup margarine, melted

1/2 box white or yellow cake mix
1/2 cup pecans, chopped

Pour pie filling into an 8x8-inch pan and sprinkle dry cake mix on top.
Pour melted margarine over cake mix and cover with nuts. Bake at 350°
for 45 minutes. 4 servings.

PEACH COBBLER

1 cup sugar
2/3 cup milk
1 cup self-rising flour

1 stick margarine
1 can peaches

In a medium bowl, mix together sugar, flour and milk until smooth. In a medium baking dish, melt a stick of margarine. Pour flour mixture over melted margarine. Do not stir. Pour peaches and syrup into the batter. Do not stir. Bake at 350° for 30 minutes. 4 to 6 servings.

LEMON SQUARES

1 cup margarine   1/2 cup powdered sugar
2 cups all-purpose flour

Mix well and pat dough into greased 9x13-inch pan. Bake at 350° for 30 minutes or until slightly browned.

4 eggs, beaten   2 cups sugar
1/2 cup lemon juice   1/4 cup all-purpose flour
1 teaspoon baking powder

Mix the ingredients together and pour over pastry. Bake 30 to 40 minutes longer at 350°. Cool slightly. Dust with powdered sugar. Cut into small squares to serve. Makes 24 squares.

PECAN SQUARES

1/2 cup margarine, melted
2 cups packed brown sugar
1 cup all-purpose flour
1/4 teaspoon salt

2 teaspoons baking powder
2 eggs
1 cup pecans, chopped
1 teaspoon vanilla extract

Combine margarine and brown sugar. Beat with mixer until well blended. Add eggs, beating well. Combine flour, baking powder and salt. Add to sugar mixture and mix well. Stir in vanilla and pecans. Spoon batter into a greased and floured 13x9x2-inch pan. Bake at 350° for 25 minutes. Let cool in pan. Cut into 2-inch squares. Yield: 2 dozen.

FRUIT PIZZA

1 (18 ounce) package
    refrigerated sugar cookie
    dough
1 (8 ounce) package cream
    cheese

1/3 cup sugar
1/2 teaspoon vanilla extract
1/2 cup orange marmalade
1 tablespoon water
Assorted fresh fruits, sliced

Slice cookies 1/8-inch thick and overlap on a 14-inch pizza pan. Bake at 375° for 12 minutes. In a medium bowl, combine the cream cheese, sugar and vanilla until creamy. Spread onto cooled cookie dough. Arrange fruit in a circle on pizza and add water to marmalade. Spread over the fruit. Chill. Assorted fruits may include bananas, grapes, kiwi, strawberries, peaches or apples. 4 to 6 servings.

CHOCOLATE KRISPIES

1 (11 1/2 ounce) package
  chocolate morsels
2 cups milk
1/2 cup margarine

1/2 cup light corn syrup
2 teaspoons vanilla extract
1 cup confectioners sugar
4 cups puffed rice cereal

Combine morsels, margarine and corn syrup in a medium saucepan. Stir over low heat until melted and smooth. Remove from heat. Stir in vanilla and sugar. Add cereal, mixing lightly until well coated. Spread evenly in a buttered 13x9x2-inch pan. Chill until firm. Cut into squares. Keep stored in refrigerator. Makes 20 squares.

BROWNIES

2 cups sugar
2 teaspoons vanilla extract
1 cup shortening
4 eggs
1 1/3 cups all-purpose flour

1/2 cup cocoa
1 teaspoon baking powder
1 teaspoon salt
1 cup nuts, chopped

Cream together sugar, vanilla, shortening and eggs. Sift together flour, cocoa, baking powder and salt. Add chopped nuts to mixture and mix by hand. Bake in a 9x13-inch pan at 350° for 25 to 30 minutes. Cool and frost.

ICING:
1/3 cup cocoa
1 box powdered sugar
1 stick margarine, melted

1/2 cup evaporated milk
1 teaspoon vanilla extract
1 cup nuts, chopped

Mix together cocoa and powdered sugar. Combine with other ingredients and mix well. Frost brownies. 10 to 12 servings.

BROWNIES DELUXE

1 cup margarine	2 cups sugar
1/2 teaspoon salt	4 eggs
1 1/2 cups all-purpose flour	3/4 cup sour cream
4 (1 ounce) squares chocolate	1 cup nuts, chopped

Grease an 11x15-inch pan. Melt margarine and chocolate together and stir in salt and sugar. Add eggs, beating well after each addition. Add flour and mix well. Stir in sour cream and nuts. Bake at 350° for 30 minutes. 6 to 8 servings.

SWEET POTATO COOKIES

1/2 cup packed brown sugar
1/2 cup sugar
1/2 cup shortening
11/2 cups all-purpose flour
1 cup sweet potatoes, cooked
   and grated

1 egg
1/4 teaspoon salt
1/2 cup nuts, chopped
1 teaspoon vanilla extract

Cream sugars and shortening. Add egg and beat well. Add flour and salt and mix well. Add potatoes, nuts and vanilla. Drop by teaspoonfuls on ungreased cookie sheet. Bake at 325° for 12 to 15 minutes. Makes 3 to 4 dozen cookies.

OLD TIME TEA CAKES

2 1/2 cups all-purpose flour
1 teaspoon baking powder
1/2 teaspoon baking soda
1 teaspoon salt
1 tablespoon buttermilk

1 cup sugar
1/2 cup margarine
1 to 2 teaspoons vanilla extract
1/4 to 1/2 teaspoon nutmeg
   and/or cinnamon

Cream together sugar and margarine, beating well. Combine other ingredients and mix with sugar mixture. Roll out and cut with cookie cutter. Bake at 350° until lightly brown. Sprinkle some sugar on top before baking to make a sugar cookie. Makes 4 dozen cookies.

CHOCOLATE CHIP OATMEAL COOKIES

1 cup sugar
1 cup packed brown sugar
1 cup margarine, softened
2 eggs
2 cups all-purpose flour
1 teaspoon soda

1 teaspoon salt
3 cups quick oatmeal
2 teaspoons vanilla extract
1 to 2 cups chocolate chips
1/2 cup nuts, if desired

Cream together sugars, margarine and eggs. Add the flour, soda and salt. By hand, stir in the oatmeal, vanilla, chocolate chips and nuts. Drop by teaspoonful on cookie sheet. Bake at 350° for 10 to 12 minutes. Makes about 4 dozen.

OATMEAL PEANUT BUTTER COOKIES

2 cups quick oatmeal
1 teaspoon baking powder
1 cup crunchy peanut butter
1 cup packed brown sugar
1/2 cup sugar
1 cup all-purpose flour

1 teaspoon soda
1 teaspoon salt
3/4 cup margarine
2 eggs
2 teaspoon vanilla extract

Stir together oats, flour, baking powder, soda and salt and set aside. In a large bowl, beat peanut butter and margarine until smooth. Beat in the sugars, eggs and vanilla. Add the flour mixture. Chill dough for at least 1 hour. Drop onto greased cookie sheet by teaspoonfuls and bake at 350° for 8 to 10 minutes. Do not overcook. Makes 6 dozen.

THIMBLE COOKIES

11/2 cups all-purpose flour
3/4 cup margarine
1/2 cup brown sugar
1/4 teaspoon salt

1 egg, separated
1/2 teaspoon vanilla extract
1 cup pecans, finely chopped

Cream margarine, sugar, egg yolk and vanilla. Add flour and salt, and mix well. Chill thoroughly. Shape dough in small balls and dip in slightly beaten egg white. Roll in nuts. Place on lightly greased cookie sheet and make thumb or thimble imprint in top of cookie. Bake at 325° for 10 minutes. Makes 2 to 3 dozen cookies.

VANILLA ICE CREAM

3 eggs
1 cup sugar
1 tablespoon vanilla extract
2 cans sweetened condensed
   milk

1/2 pint whipping cream
Cold milk

Combine eggs, cream, sugar and vanilla in bowl and mix thoroughly with mixer. Add condensed milk and mix well. Pour ingredients into can and fill to fill-line with regular milk. Stir well. Yields: 4 quarts.

ORANGE SHERBET

1 (2 liter) orange drink
1 can sweetened condensed milk

1 small can crushed pineapple

Mix drink with milk well. Put in ice cream freezer and freeze until almost frozen. Add pineapple and continue to freeze. Yields: 4 quarts.

PEACH ICE CREAM

7 cups peaches
3 cups milk, divided
2 large eggs, lightly beaten
2 1/2 cups sugar

1 (12 ounce) can evaporated
  milk
1 (12 ounce) can peach nectar

Combine half of peaches and 1/4 cup milk in the blender; process until smooth. Pour this mixture into a medium bowl and repeat the procedure. Set aside. In a heavy saucepan, over medium heat, cook the 2 1/2 cups milk, eggs, evaporated milk and sugar, for 8 minutes, stirring occasionally. Remove from the heat and stir in peach mixture and nectar. Pour mixture into a 4-quart freezer container and freeze. Freeze mixture according to freezer instructions. Pack freezer with additional ice and rock salt and let stand for 30 minutes before serving. Yield: 4 quarts.

NOTES

NOTES

NOTES

NOTES

MAIN DISHES

Does your organization need a fund raiser -
Try our Little Keepsake

*EZ-L BAK
COOKBOOKS*

We have stock cookbooks or
You can design your own!!